THE

BLUEPRINT

To Manifest Your Dreams

Mariko Bennett

Published by Coco B. Productions in the United States of America.

First printing, 2021.

ISBN: 978-1-7367089-0-3
www.marikobennett.com

This book is dedicated to my tribe.

To my beautiful children, who push and challenge me to be a better person daily.

To my husband, who supports every idea I have.

To my mother, who is my role model.

To my father, who instilled my 'never quit' attitude and keeps me accountable.

To my friends, who lift me up; It's the take-over ladies!

Thank you for loving and supporting me.

ACKNOWLEDGEMENTS

I would like to extend a very special thank you to:

CopyThat Consulting and Kimberly Rodgers, who translated my work, notes and vision into organized chapters.

Ashaki Brown for ensuring that my book was perfectly packaged and ready for prime time.

Mike Duncan for his creative genius on designing my book cover.

Jacqueline & Erick Sellman, the make-up and photography dream team.

Justin Marcel for keeping my hair laid!

Michele Lopez for ensuring that I "Showed Up" in my fullness and told my authentic story of who I am through my images.

Foreword

Regardless of how you define it, success – whether in the workplace or in personal life – is something we all dream about. It's easy and natural to spend time imagining what it would feel like to positively transform your organizational culture, get that promotion, pay off that debt, or take that trip of a lifetime. But dreaming is just the beginning; what comes next, carving out a path toward your success, is what matters most. Dreams paint a pretty picture of what success looks like, but you need strategic goals to make that picture come to life.

Throughout my 30-plus years at a Fortune 10 company, goal-setting has propelled me up the ranks from an account executive to executive leadership. The ability to take a vision or idea, develop a goal-driven plan, and pinpoint concrete action steps to move it forward is one of my most coveted assets. That invaluable skill is how I have delivered value to my organization and colleagues for over three decades and how I found success in my personal life. Goal-setting is an acquired skill that I was fortunate to learn early in my career but for many this task may seem daunting. This dynamic book aims to change that.

From beginning to end, Mariko Bennett distills the components of goal-setting in a way that is both motivating and fun. The book makes clear the difference between a dream and a goal; going beyond just describing the process to provide tools and templates that allow you to immediately apply the concepts and transform your unique vision into reality. By equipping you to establish goals that are specific, measurable, achievable, relevant and time-bound (SMART), this book is exactly what you need to cast your vision and make it plain.

I can't wait to apply the principles within to my personal goals, and as a human resources executive, I'm already thinking of ways to introduce this book into my organization. Not only will it support our leadership in setting and aligning strategic goals that move the company forward, it will be incredibly useful in helping staff develop clear and actionable performance goals — and it can do the same for you. Whether you want to find success through short-term personal wins or longer-term professional accomplishments, this book is the blueprint you need.

Gail Coles Johnson
Assistant Vice President, Human Resources
AT&T

TESTIMONIAL OF CREATE THE BLUEPRINT VISION BOARD EXPERIENCE

I am a living testimony that your wildest dreams and vision for your life really can come true. It's no understatement when I say the manifestation of my life's dreams and vision are directly explained from the success of Mariko's *'Create The Blueprint Vision Board Experience.'* They are predicated on the inner potential she cultivated within me. Through Mariko's coaching, I embraced my goals and primed intentional imagining to believe that all things are possible. Here are the receipts: I attended one of her events in January, that allowed successful women to collaborate, communicate, and celebrate their vision in seven life-focus areas. I focused on a professional vision that would land me a new career with trusted and honorable corporate leadership; that aligns with my personal values; pays a six-figure salary; where I will grow with colleagues deliberate about an environment of mutual respect and admiration; and a place that I will successfully deliver on the job responsibilities. In the beginning of February of the same year, I was offered an opportunity of a lifetime to onboard at Walgreens Boots Alliance! There's more. One week after that opportunity, I received a call to audition and interview as a volunteer monthly host for *Seniors Today* - a local county cable program produced by Comcast. The dreams and vision I have for my life were cultivated at *'Create The Blueprint Vision Board Experience.'* I can certainly be, because Mariko helped me see!

Katie Smith

THE PATH TO YOUR DREAMS

Introduction
A Message to Dreamers

Section I
Design the Life You Want

Life isn't a spectator sport. The universe can't magically manifest your dreams. But with the power of visualization and the keys to manifestation, you can.

Section II
Crystallize Your Vision

Your dreams may be broad, but your vision should be focused.
Make yourself a priority and reflect on what you want from life so you can set intentions that help you become your best self.

Section III
Customize Your Approach

When you fail to prepare, you prepare to fail. Set SMART goals, anticipate obstacles, and analyze your resources so you can be strategic and manifest your goals with precision.

Section IV

Cultivate Your Vision

You've got to believe it to achieve it. Create a vision board that empowers you to stay focused on your dreams. Remember to make time to affirm yourself. You can and will succeed.

Section V

Curate Your Dreams

Your dreams don't work unless you do. Learn how to move from dreaming to doing and track your progress.

A Final Word

INTRO

A Message to Dreamers

Dear Dreamer,

We all have dreams; visions of our best selves living our best lives. We see ourselves getting that promotion, finding love, or taking flight for a bucket list trip. These moments spent dreaming feel good. They offer a reminder of what's possible, filling us with hope and purpose. And yet, for many people, dreams end where they start – in our heads.

For so many reasons, dreams can feel far-fetched or out of reach. Maybe you feel undeserving or like you're asking the universe for too much. Maybe you get stuck thinking about the obstacles and barriers you might face. Or maybe you just don't know where or how to begin your journey. However, if you want to manifest your dreams, you need to free yourself from the burden of all those doubts and what-ifs.

It's not easy. I'm living proof of that.

I spent years dreaming about entrepreneurship, contemplating the pros and cons. There were countless moments where I wasn't sure it would be the right decision. Leaving corporate America to start my own business meant giving up my stable income, benefits package, and corporate perks from a Fortune 500 company. It meant making up-front sacrifices in the name of long-term successes. But ultimately, **the risk was worth it** because it meant that I believed in myself enough to take a chance on me.

Now, four years after making that leap, I find myself in a position where I'm my own boss. I bet on myself and my wildest dream is now my everyday reality. I set my own hours, choose the clients I want to work with, and have the time and financial stability to engage in more initiatives that benefit the global community. I'm living my best life and it feels amazing.

Many people will hear a story like mine, where a leap of faith turned a lifelong vision into reality, and say, *"That's great, but it seems more like the exception than the rule."* But it doesn't have to be. I firmly believe that with the right guidance, structure, and resources, everyone has the capacity to achieve their dreams. That's why I wrote this book – I want to help people do just that.

This is an invitation to dream. To feel confident enough to claim your dreams. To boldly turn them into reality.

It's an invitation to envision your best life—one where you're living your purpose, following your passions, and feeling love and support.

It's an invitation to design a plan to manifest your vision. To transform yourself in whatever ways you want to be transformed. To align yourself with experiences, people, and things that enrich your life.

Grounded in the principles of visualization and SMART goal setting, this workbook encourages you to dream and be strategic about pursuing those dreams.

What follows within is a guide to the Four C's of manifestation: **crystallizing** your dreams into a clear vision, **customizing** a strategic approach that positions you for success, **cultivating** your vision through the power of vision boarding, and **curating** your best life through action. Each chapter features a short discussion along with some self-guided exercises that invite you to reflect upon and practically apply the principles of the Four C's to help you manifest your goals.

I'm excited for you to start this journey – and blessed to be able to guide you. The process won't always be smooth or easy, but changing yourself and your life rarely is. Embrace the struggle, celebrate the small wins, and remember that even when you stumble on your journey, you can get back up, dust yourself off, and try again.

Your dreams are waiting. Let's go get them.

Love,

Mariko Bennett

Do something today that your future self will thank you for.

Design the Life You Want

THE POWER OF VISUALIZATION

RHONDA
BYRNE

"The law of attraction is forming your entire life experience and it is doing that through your thoughts. When you are visualizing, you are emitting a powerful frequency out into the Universe."
— Rhonda Byrne, author of best-selling book *The Secret*

Most people have envisioned what their ideal lives would look like. For some, that might include a corner office at a corporate job and a penthouse apartment. Others are drawn to the freedom of ownership, so they imagine what it would be like to buy their first home or start a small business. And for others, the aspiration may be even more personal, like focusing on sustaining supportive and loving relationships with family and friends. But for so many people, those visions end right where they begin – compartmentalized in the mind as something that sounds nice but exists just out of reach. In reality, the visualization of these things is actually the first step toward something greater.

Visualization is one of the most powerful mind exercises you can do. This concept became popular in the 1970s after Soviet scientists discovered that athletes who spent seventy-five percent of their time engaged in mental visualization and twenty-five percent of their time in physical training actually performed better than athletes who spent more time in physical training.[1] For years, visualization has been a staple among elite athletes, such as Tiger Woods[2] and Olympic gold medalists Katie Ledecky and Michael Phelps.[3] Today, the practice is even more common and is frequently used outside of sports circles by people ranging from Fortune 500 CEOs to stay-at-home parents. It might seem far-fetched that just visualizing something you want will help manifest it, but it works. As *New York Times* best-selling author and Oprah's *SuperSoul100* visionary Shawn Achor once put it, "Vivid pictures are like magnets pulling us toward a better future."

---

[1] Robert Scaglione and William Cummins, *Karate of Okinawa: Building Warrior Spirit* (New York: Person-to-Person Publishing, Inc., 1990).
[2] John Andrisani, *Think Like Tiger: An Analysis of Tiger Woods's Mental Game* (New York: G.P. Putnam's Sons, 2002).
[3] Rovello, Jessica, "5 Ways Katie Ledecky, Michael Phelps, and Other Olympians Visualize Success," *Inc.*, August 23, 2016, www.inc.com/jessica-rovello/five-steps-to-visualize-success-like-an-olympian.html.

Now, let's be clear, the act of visualization in itself is not enough to get you closer to your goals. You still have to do the work. However, visualization is a critical tool that helps you transition from thinking to doing. In 2007, neuroscientist and researcher Tali Sharot and colleagues published a study in the prestigious academic journal *Nature*, which found that detailed visualizations of success can trigger our brains to feel the positive emotions that come with achievement and, in turn, motivate us to take action.[4]

Nearly a decade later, a survey by TD Bank discovered that people who visualize their goals are more confident about — and more successful in — achieving their vision. The survey found that seventy-six percent of small business owners who used vision boarding – a visualization tactic that involves attaching words and images to a board to create a physical representation of your vision – reported that their business actually reflected what they originally envisioned. Of those who used vision boarding at the outset of their business, 82% had accomplished more than half the goals on their vision board.[5] Even for skeptics, it's hard to argue with such results. Plus, some of the most successful people swear by the power of visualization!

I had never had a vision board before. I came home, I got me a board, put Barack Obama's picture on it, and I put a picture of my dress I want to wear to the inauguration."
– Oprah Winfrey, on doing her first vision board after an Obama campaign rally

Everything I've ever gotten in life, I've written. My vision board is crazy. What's on my board now is astronomical, and guess what? I'm gonna get all of it."
– Steve Harvey, on manifesting success

---

[4] Achor, Shawn, "The Power of Visualization," *Success*, October 10, 2019, https://www.success.com/the-power-of-visualization.
[5] Zimmerman, Eilene, "Survey shows Visualizing Success Works," *Forbes*, January 27, 2016, https://www.forbes.com/sites/eilenezimmerman/2016/01/27/survey-shows-visualizing-success-works/#296113bd760b.

ELLEN DEGENERES

You have to put it out in the universe, and it'll come to you. You gotta have a dream.
– Ellen DeGeneres, on adding the cover of O, *The Oprah Magazine* to her vision board

DENZEL WASHINGTON

You attract what you feel, what you are, what's on your mind.
– Denzel Washington, on the law of attraction

JIM CARREY

"I would visualize having directors interested in me and people I respected saying 'I like your work.' I would visualize things coming me to that I wanted.
– Jim Carrey, on life before fame

The Bottom Line: Visualization helps you see your dreams in 3D. It's a widely-used and effective technique that will help you imagine the life you want, motivate you to take control, and prepare you to design your own achievement and success.

THE KEYS TO MANIFESTATION

Visualization is a powerful tool because it allows you to focus on your dreams and picture the possibilities of your life. You can't be what you can't see. Envisioning a new reality gives you a chance to imagine what it might feel like and empowers you to believe it's possible.

Your dreams don't work unless you do.

However, visualization alone isn't enough. You must be willing to do the work. The door to your dreams won't open itself – you have to unlock it with the key to manifestation: The **Four C's** (C-POWER)

When applied with passion, persistence, and discipline, the Four C's – **crystallize, customize, cultivate,** and **curate** – will help you move your vision off your board and into your real life. Every time I've had a dream and set goals to get there, the Four C's have been my secret weapon and the building blocks to my success. Today, they also become yours.

CP1 = CRYSTALLIZE

Solidify your vision. Whether you want to increase your sales or get in better shape, this phase is where you paint the big picture of what you want to achieve.

CP2 = CUSTOMIZE

Craft your plan. Your vision may be broad, but you'll need to narrow your focus into concrete goals and secure the resources needed to achieve them.

CP3 = CULTIVATE

Set yourself up for success. When life gets crazy, it's easy to lose sight of your goals. However, with the help of your vision board and a solid affirmation routine, you can keep your eyes on the prize.

CP4 = CURATE

Execute with confidence. With your vision, plan, and resources mapped out, it's time to make it happen!

This workbook will walk you through each of the Four C's. As you learn how to crystallize, customize, cultivate, and curate your vision and dreams, you will gain the "c-power" needed to help you see your power. Not only will this help you be more deliberate, strategic, and intentional about your goals, it will also help you stay motivated and accountable as you execute your vision with precision.

The Bottom Line: Your vision is just a blueprint – it won't work unless you act. As much as I wish I could offer a shortcut to your dreams, I can't because there isn't one. You have to be willing to strategize a path to success, make necessary sacrifices to stay on that path, and sustain behaviors that move you closer to your end goal. This is what I can help you with, this is what I'm here to do, and it all starts with the **Four C's.**

CRYSTALLIZE

YOUR

VISION

Focus on You

"Create the highest, grandest vision possible for your life, because you become what you believe." – Oprah Winfrey

When creating a vision for your life, the first step is to dream big and out loud. But let's be real – that's easier said than done, especially when it's hard to make time for yourself. I don't know about you, but I feel like I'm constantly on the move, juggling a million things. There's so much to think about each day that I sometimes get lost in it all. *What does my family need? When is that work thing due? Did I double-book my social calendar again?* It's easy to get caught in a cycle of focusing so much on others that you forget to think about yourself.

I'm sure you can relate.

While it's good to give attention to others and take care of the people and things that matter, you can't forget to pay attention to yourself. We sometimes get so enmeshed in the labels we carry — parent, partner, friend, boss, employee — that we lose our individuality. However, it's important to remember that you're more than those things; you're a person with dreams and aspirations, and it's necessary to focus on what you want, too. Allowing yourself to dream is a good place to start.

Dreams are powerful because they give us a chance to imagine the best version of ourselves and our lives. They give us a glimpse of what's possible and a vision to work toward. But your dreams must come with a dose of faith. You have to believe that you're capable of transforming them into reality. I know it's a cliché, but I strongly stand by the mantra that "if you can believe it, you can achieve it." As I like to put it, "You've got to name what you want to claim what you want."

I thought about leaving corporate America for quite some time before I actually did so. I was ready to branch out on my own and be my own boss, but I was worried about what would happen if entrepreneurship wasn't immediately fruitful. I kept waiting, hoping that the time would be right, before it finally hit me: *what if the time was never 'right?'* I couldn't keep waiting for the universe to magically align everything for me. I had to make my own magic.

I started visualizing what it would be like to run the business of my dreams and then practiced my vision in my personal life. I turned family vacations and girls' trips into an opportunity to flex my event-planning muscles. I used my kids' school fundraisers to practice different donor relations strategies. I tracked leadership trends to identify what kinds of coaching and training would be in demand. I hosted free vision board parties for local nonprofits.

I was doing things I enjoyed that didn't feel like work and finding ways to focus on my vision. I was staying connected to my dream while I waited for an opportunity to seize it.

Your dream may not come as quickly or easily as you'd like, but you can't be deterred. Hold tight to it. Write it down. Speak it out loud. Believe in it. Your dream is a reflection of you – treat it how you want to be treated.

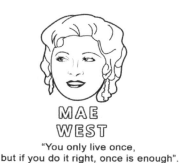

MAE
WEST
"You only live once,
but if you do it right, once is enough".

— Mae West, *actress, singer, screenwriter, and comedian*

The Bottom Line: We all have dreams as young people. Then life happens and sometimes we stop dreaming. Don't allow your dreams to become an afterthought. Instead, make them a priority. Get back to dreaming. It's your opportunity to better understand who you want to be and what you want to get out of this life. So dream! Give yourself the chance to envision a better, more fulfilling, and more enjoyable existence. There are already enough obstacles standing between you and what you want in this world. Don't hold yourself back by forgetting to focus on your most important priority – you.

Self(ish) Reflection

Growing up, my father always told me, "Put your oxygen mask on first"; a reminder that your existence – your happiness, your fulfillment, your wellness – sometimes hinges on you being selfish for a moment. So try it! Use these questions to do some self(ish) reflection.

• How are the key parts of your life – family/friends, work, hobbies, financial stability, romantic relationships, etc. – affecting your physical, mental, emotional, and/or spiritual well-being? What changes could you make for the sake of your well-being?

• What are you grateful for?

• What feels challenging right now? What are you struggling with?

Self(ish) Reflection

• What are your values? Do you feel like you stay to true to them? How so?

• What is your purpose – your 'why'? If you're not sure, how does it feel to be figuring it out?

• What would you do if you weren't afraid of anything, including judgment or consequences?

• What is your wildest dream?

CONCEPTUALIZE YOUR VISION

My Intentions

- Live a healthier life.
    - o   Lose weight, eat out less, exercise, meditate
- Get a promotion.
    - o   Complete a certification, lead a project
- Spend more time with family and friends.
    - o   Host game nights or dinners, set dates for video chats

---

You know yourself and what you want best, so your vision should be yours and yours alone. As you consider what you want it to include, it's okay to think big or outside of the box. This isn't the time to limit yourself – it's the time to believe that anything is possible. You will refine your vision and customize a plan for achieving it a little later. For now, put all your aspirations on the table.

Start by making a list of intentions you want to incorporate into your vision. Again, you don't have to get super specific just yet. Then, under each of those intentions, list slightly more specific aims that help you narrow your intentions into basic goals. Here's an example:

Starting with a broad intention gives you the freedom to think about what that intention really means to *you*. Two people could have the same intention but be seeking very different outcomes. For example, one person may measure living a healthier life by some physical standard (e.g. losing weight) while another may measure it by a mental health standard (e.g. increasing mindfulness). This process of starting with a big picture and then refining it serves to help you pinpoint exactly how to crystallize your vision to reflect the changes you want to see in your life.

Let's take a second to set your vision by starting with the big picture. Think about what you envision for your life, then use the blank space to write down what intentions capture your vision. Later, you will transform these intentions into concrete goals that will help you achieve your vision

Believe In Yourself

State Your Intentions

CP2

CUSTOMIZE

YOUR

APPROACH

From Intention to Action:
Setting SMART Goals

Intentions are only aspirations, so now it's time to make them actionable. To do this, you need to transform your intentions into SMART goals. SMART goals are specific, measurable, achievable, relevant, and time-bound.

Specific – *What do you want to accomplish with this goal?*

Your vision can be broad, but your goals should be focused. Identifying exactly what you want to accomplish allows you to pursue your goals more intentionally. Be specific about what you want to achieve with each goal. For example:

- *Increase revenue by ten percent in the first quarter.*
- *Exercise four days per week for at least thirty minutes.*
- *Find a new job that improves my work-life balance.*

Measurable – *How will you know you've hit your goal?*

To monitor progress, your goals need a benchmark. The metrics you use to measure your goal can be quantitative or qualitative. Quantitative metrics consider how many, how much, or how often (e.g. increase revenue by ten percent) while qualitative metrics assess quality (e.g. improve work-life balance).

- *Increase revenue **by ten percent** in the first quarter.*
- *Exercise **four days per week** for **at least thirty minutes**.*
- *Find a new job that **improves my work-life balance.***

Achievable – *Is your goal realistic?*

Setting unrealistic goals is a good way to fail. An unrealistic goal requires you to give more – time, energy, resources – than you currently have or can reasonably access. Your goals should push you, but not sabotage the journey to your vision before it even begins. Set goals that can be achieved with the resources that are available or attainable.

Relevant – *Will this goal help you manifest your vision?*

Think of your goals as stepping stones that set the path toward your vision. When the goals are relevant, the path is more direct, making it easier and faster to get to your vision. Irrelevant goals can throw you off course, resulting in false starts and wasted resources. Avoid this by making sure your goals support – and move you closer to – your vision.

Time-Bound – *When will you achieve this goal?*

It's important to know by when you want to achieve a goal. Setting a deadline helps you map out how long you have to work toward the goal and set benchmarks to track progress. For example, if it's January and you want to lose ten pounds by April, you know you have four months to meet your goal and you can create a plan to lose 2.5 pounds per month. Time-bound goals help to facilitate both planning and accountability.

Goals are dreams with deadlines.

IT'S GOAL-SETTING TIME!

With your intentions as inspiration, develop a set of SMART goals. There is no perfect number; you should have enough goals to help you achieve the various aspects of your vision, but not so many that you can't reasonably pursue all of them. To help keep your set of goals tight and focused, ask yourself: *Do my goals support my vision? Are my goals duplicative? Are any of my goals in conflict with another one? What obstacles might I face?*

Remember, these goals are your stepping stones to success. Each one should position you to manifest your vision. Write your goals in the space below.

My Goals

OWN YOUR OBSTACLES

Too little time. Competing priorities. Lack of discipline. Low confidence. Each of us carries our own burden of obstacles that have kept us from achieving the things we say we want. When obstacles are out of our control, we tend to see them more clearly. However, we often have a hard time acknowledging the obstacles that we create for ourselves.

Part of my vision every year includes an intention to get healthier. A couple of years ago for one of my 'get healthier' goals, I told myself in January that I wanted to lose ten pounds by the end of March. But when March 31st rolled around, I was actually five pounds heavier than when I set my goal. I was frustrated and began reflecting on how and why I didn't succeed.

At first, I put the blame on work. Running Coco B. Productions was so time-intensive, from developing proposals to building relationships and putting on events, that I was exhausted at the end of each day. As a result, I found myself skipping the gym and grabbing takeout for lunch and dinner more often than not. I let myself believe that the realities of entrepreneurship presented obstacles that were simply out of my control. But they were only out of my control because I failed to adapt to them.

Even after realizing that my schedule was stretched thin with client meetings, pitches, and networking events, I never tried to adapt to my new reality. Instead of meal-prepping on the weekends so I could have healthy lunches on the go and nutritious dinners waiting at home after long days, I chose to settle for eating out. Instead of waking up early to exercise before I got swept up in work, I kept telling myself I'd do it at the end of the day, even though I knew I'd be too tired. I made excuses. *I'll make changes starting next week*, I thought.

Before I knew it, there was only one week left in March. My failure to prepare prepared me to fail. It was disappointing, but I learned an important lesson. While I couldn't control the intensity of my work life, I could have adjusted my approach to taking care of myself in the midst of the chaos. That realization changed everything, and when I set a new goal to lose the now-fifteen pounds by the end of June, I understood my personal obstacles well enough to overcome them.

I changed my eating habits, cutting out foods that I knew weren't good for my body. I started meal-prepping on Sundays so that I had ready-to-eat meals throughout the week. I built workouts into my daily schedule, adding them as protected appointments on my calendar so that I wouldn't need to cancel due to conflicting meetings. I hired a personal trainer who could help me maximize the efficiency of my sweat sessions. I kept a couple of spare sets of workout gear in my car in case I ever forgot my gym bag. I did what I could to eliminate the factors that slowed me down the first time. I owned my obstacles and reached my goal in mid-June.

MICHAEL JORDAN

"If you're trying to achieve,
there will be roadblocks.
But obstacles don't have to stop you.
If you run into a wall,
don't turn around and give up.
Figure out how to climb it, go through it
or work around it."

— Michael Jordan, six-time NBA champion and two-time inductee of the Naismith Memorial Basketball Hall of Fame

The Bottom Line: We all stumble on our journey to something greater. When you can predict and acknowledge your obstacles, especially the ones you self-create, you become better positioned to control what you can and make changes that help you overcome barriers. By identifying where you've fallen short in the past, you can course-correct in the present to know what traps to watch out for and what areas of personal growth to focus on. Sacrifices will most certainly be required, but those sacrifices are simply stepping stones to reaching your goals.

What's in the Way?

Think of some of the goals you've set for yourself throughout your life. Which of these obstacles have you struggled to overcome in pursuit of your goals? Circle the ones that apply or use the extra space to write in any others you want to add.

Lack of skill	Lack of patience	Lack of discipline
Lack of knowledge	Lack of inspiration	Lack of resources
Fear of change	Fear of failure	Complacency
Feeling unworthy	Procrastination	Perfectionism
Pessimistic thoughts	Time constraints	Excuses

How have these obstacles kept you from achieving goals previously?

Considering the goals you've just set, which of these obstacles are you most concerned about?

If a friend was experiencing those obstacles, what advice would you share to motivate them to keep going?

Assess Your Resources

In the first part of the book, I encouraged you to focus on yourself. Now it's time to turn your attention outward and consider what – and who – will help you make your vision come true. It's time to think about the resources you have and the ones you need. There are several main types to consider:

Physical. Physical resources are tangible assets. These could include buildings and facilities, equipment and machinery, or software.

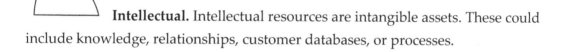

Intellectual. Intellectual resources are intangible assets. These could include knowledge, relationships, customer databases, or processes.

Human. Human resources are the people you need. Depending on what your vision entails, this might include employees, mentors, lawyers, training professionals, etc.

Financial. Financial resources are the monetary assets you need. Depending on what your goals are, you may not need every type of resource. To determine what you need, consider the following:

- Which types of resources do I need (e.g. physical, intellectual, human, financial)?
- Within each type, what resources do I already have and what resources do I still need?

- Of the resources I still need, which ones do I know how and where to obtain? Which needed resources will require me to do research about where to obtain them?

ARTHUR ASHE

"Start where you are,
use what you have, do what you can."

— Arthur Ashe, *first and only Black male tennis player to win the U.S. Open and Wimbledon singles titles*

DO YOUR HOMEWORK

Once you've determined what resources you need, try doing some research about where to get those resources.

For example, if you want to launch a new business venture, you could check out resources from the Small Business Administration and National Federation of Independent Businesses, or from location or sector-based grant programs available specifically for your city or line of business.

Alternatively, say you need a meal-planning service – look online into which of the many available options is best for your taste, dietary needs, and budget.

Don't be afraid to think outside the box, too. If there's a resource you need but may not be able to afford, consider bartering or setting up a *quid pro quo* that allows you to trade your own skills and resources – your superpowers – in exchange for those that you need. Not only is this a means to get the resources to support your goals, but it also allows you to build a support network of professionals and creatives that you can collaborate with in the future.

LENA WAITHE
"The things that make us different, those are our superpowers."

— Lena Waithe, *Emmy Award-winning screenwriter, producer, and actress*

You're super. Embrace your power.

You have a lot to offer — and so does your circle of influence, which could include coworkers, friends and family, neighbors, even people you've met at networking events. Use these questions to map out the assets (superpowers!) that you and your circle of influence bring to the table, and consider how you could support each other in reaching your goals.

What are your superpowers? What skills, perspective, or expertise do you bring to the table?

Think about the people in your circle of influence and networks. What are some of the superpowers they have? What do they bring to the table that you could use?

How can you unite your superpowers with those of your circle of influence to help uplift each other and transform yourselves into the super people you envision in your dreams?

Beyond figuring out how to fill your resource gaps, it's also important to explore what success has typically looked like for people who've already achieved what you're setting out to accomplish. So much knowledge and so many lessons exist in the minds and experiences of those who have walked the path that you're just setting out on. There's no need to feel like you're on this journey alone or that you have to reinvent the wheel to get where you're going. Use the experiences and recommendations of others to your benefit.

Just remember that even though it's tempting to fixate on how super successful people – like, Beyoncé-level successful – got to where they are, you can't forget to seek out the stories of people whose standard of living and access to resources is similar to yours. Find opportunities to connect with accessible people who've experienced success, and have practical conversations with them about what worked, what didn't, and what advice they might have.

The Bottom Line: When you fail to prepare, you prepare to fail. By identifying what you need to go after your goals, you increase your potential to achieve them. Assess your resources, identify your strengths and acknowledge your gaps, do your homework to fill gaps, and position yourself to be successful.

What I Have vs. What I Need

Referencing your goals on page 30, use the following pages to write each goal down and inventory your resources.

Goal 1	
I have...	**I need...**

I feel confident that...

I might face some obstacles, such as...

To overcome those obstacles, I plan to...

Goal 2

I have...	I need...

I feel confident that...

I might face some obstacles, such as...

To overcome those obstacles, I plan to...

Goal 3

| |
| |

I have...	I need...

I feel confident that...

I might face some obstacles, such as...

To overcome those obstacles, I plan to...

Goal 4

I have...	I need...

I feel confident that...

I might face some obstacles, such as...

To overcome those obstacles, I plan to...

Goal 5

I have...	I need...

I feel confident that...

I might face some obstacles, such as...

To overcome those obstacles, I plan to...

I Love
And Accept
Myself
As I Am
Right Now!

CULTIVATE

YOUR

VISION

Keep Your Eye on the Prize:
The Art of Vision Boarding

The busier and crazier life gets, the harder it can be to stay focused on your vision. That's why creating a vision board is so important. It captures the vision you have for your best life and serves as a visual reminder of the goals you've set to fulfill that vision. Plus, it's a great tool for staying encouraged and accountable. It's hard to run from your vision when it's staring you in the face every day!

Vision boarding involves creating a collage that represents what you want to attract, create, and achieve in your life. The visuals on your vision board should speak to what's most important and meaningful for you. They should evoke a strong sense of emotion that sparks you to not just think but also *feel* what it would be like to see your vision come to fruition.

If you've already created your vision board, you can skip to the next section. Otherwise, get ready to get crafty!

To create your vision board, you'll need a poster or cork board, visual materials (e.g. magazines, photos, stickers), scissors, markers, glue sticks or push pins, and – most importantly – your vision.

CREATE YOUR VISION BOARD

Follow these steps to map your vision onto your vision board.

Step 1: Piece Together a Picture of Success

With your vision and goals in mind, think about what success looks like to you.

- What do you see?
- Who comes to mind?
- Which feelings or emotions come up?

Answering these questions will help you pick the right mix of words, images, photos, or other items to put on your board.

Step 2: Create Your Vision Board

Now it's time to gather the visual representations of your vision. Using photos, magazine clippings, computer printouts, and any other materials you like, compile the images, quotes, and words that reflect your vision; and depict a picture of success. Attach them to your vision board in a way that resonates with you. A great resource tool to assist you in this is *Create The Blueprint Clip Art, Quotes, and Words By Mariko Bennett.*

You might want to include visuals that compare where you are today with where you want to be, representing your transformation. Perhaps you want every visual to be accompanied by an uplifting phrase or quote. However, you go about it, just remember that your board is a tool to help you continuously see, feel, and touch your vision so that you stay inspired to do the work.

Step 3: Put Your Vision in View

When your vision board is complete, display it somewhere you'll see it every day. That could be the wall of your bathroom, your home office, or your kitchen—wherever makes the most sense for you. Placing your board in an accessible place helps you keep your eye on the prize. It also minimizes the chance that your vision and goals will fade into the background once the real, hard work to reach them starts.

Celebrate! You're One Step Closer.

Finishing your vision board is just one step in the beginning of your journey to achieve your goals and manifest your vision. But it's a big step. You've created the blueprint to help you manifest your dreams. Take a moment to celebrate the commitment you've made so far – you deserve it!

How does it feel to have your vision mapped out?

Where do you plan to put your board?

What are you most looking forward to on this journey?

ADVANCE WITH AFFIRMATION

RALPH WALDO
EMERSON
"The ancestor of every action
is a thought."

– Ralph Waldo Emerson, philosopher and poet

There's a reason that people say "practice makes perfect" —there's power in repetition. Doing the same action over and over again builds mastery. As important as it is to become a master of the actions that will help you fulfill your goals, it's just as important to master how you think about those actions. The whole idea behind visualization is that we become what we think, so mastery of thought is critical to success. What you want to become is already outlined in your vision, so use the power of thought to affirm that you're capable of turning your vision into reality. An easy way to do this is to create an affirmation routine.

Affirmations are words of encouragement that foster faith, confidence, and self-efficacy – characteristics that sustain your belief in your goals and your vision. When repeated over time, affirmations help you overcome negative thoughts and create self-assurance that you are capable and worthy of reaching your goals. You can create your own affirmations or, if you're not sure where to start, search for some online.

Here are a few affirmations I've used before:

I AM POWERFUL

I DESERVE WELLNESS

I AM COMMITTED
TO THE PROCESS

I SEE MY VISION
CLEARLY

I KNOW WHAT IT TAKES
TO ACHIEVE IT

I AM DISCIPLINED

I AM FOCUSED

I DESERVE SUCCESS

I DESERVE MY HAPPINESS

I AM DETERMINED

Once you have a set of affirmations that work for you, consider creating a routine for affirming yourself. You might decide that you want to recite a certain affirmation at a certain time of day. This is a good way to integrate positivity and reassurance throughout the day to carry you through whatever obligations or obstacles arise. For example:

Daily Affirmation Routine

- **Wake-Up:** I am focused. I am strong. I am powerful. My vision will become reality.
- **Mid-Day:** I see my vision clearly. I know what it takes to achieve it. I am committed to the process.
- **Before Bed:** I deserve happiness. I deserve wellness. I deserve success. What is for me will be for me.

You may also want another list of affirmations that you can use when you're dealing with a particular emotion.

Affirmation Routine to Balance Emotions

- **When in doubt:** My goals matter because I matter. The work might be hard, but I am worth it.
- **When overwhelmed:** I control my thoughts. I control my actions. I control my life. I can do this.

Just like your vision and your goals, your affirmation routine should reflect your reality. Create a routine that works with your motivational style and schedule so that you stick to it. You could set parameters for how many times you recite your affirmations each day or decide to affirm yourself at certain intervals (e.g. every three hours). The possibilities are endless – you just need to determine what works for you.

The Bottom Line: Affirming yourself is a critical part of staying focused and confident on your journey to achieving your goals. Creating an affirmation routine will help you celebrate moments of triumph and remain hopeful during moments when you're struggling to stay on track.

My Affirmation Routine

Develop an affirmation routine that works for your lifestyle, schedule, and motivational style. If it helps, consider writing your affirmations on sticky notes and placing them where you spend the most time (e.g. home, work, vehicle).

CURATE

YOUR

DREAMS

GET TO WORK

Right about now, you probably feel pretty good – and you should! The journey to this point has been fun and exciting. How often do we give ourselves time and space to just dream—to focus on things that would make our lives more meaningful, more fulfilling, and more prosperous? To be intentional about pursuing those things? There's something incredibly invigorating about it all.

THOMAS EDISON
"Vision without execution is hallucination."

-Thomas Alva Edison was an American inventor and businessman who has been described as America's greatest inventor

But there's a time for dreaming and a time for doing, and now it's time to DO. You've already crystallized your vision, customized your plan, and cultivated a process to see it all through. The only thing left to do is get to work curating your dreams.

For many people, this phase of the process is the hardest because it demands change. Everything before this was highlighted by the *idea* or *possibility* of change, but this is where you must decide to make the change happen. As you work toward your goals, you may need to alter a behavior, adopt a new habit, or shift your daily routine. You may also have to give up some things, like time, money, or your favorite mouth-watering but oh-so-unhealthy food. Lastly, it's a harsh truth, but you may also have to separate yourself from any people who are distracting you from your journey or are just flat-out unsupportive.

None of those things are easy. Along the way, your diligence, fortitude, and commitment will be tested. There will be times when you feel overwhelmed or like you're lacking control. Maybe your progress plateaued or you took a step backward on your journey. As frustrating as this could feel, guess what? You're human! The missteps, wrong turns, stumbles – are all a normal part of the process. Instead of folding in the face of failure, this is when you need to fight the hardest to hang on to your vision.

VALERIE JARRETT

"If you have the good fortune to have a choice,
you can keep trying to do what you have always done,
or you can listen to the most important voice
—the voice inside of you. Listen to it,
and give yourself permission to swerve."

-Valerie June Jarrett is an American businesswoman and former politician. She served as senior adviser (2009–17) to U.S. President Barack Obama.

The Bottom Line: I've said it before and I'll say it again: your dreams don't work unless you do. Turning your dreams into reality won't happen overnight. Manifesting your vision is a long game, so gear yourself up for it. Commit yourself to the process, fight the urge to take shortcuts, and don't give up when things inevitably get hard. There will be tough moments, but you're tougher. Never forget that.

REPEAT AFTER ME

As you adapt your life to support your goals, all the change required may feel overwhelming. Stay grounded by reciting the note below — a quick reminder of why you're on this journey of manifestation. I like to read each stanza to myself and then say it out loud to speak it into the universe. You try it.

When things get hard...
I will push through. I know my dreams don't work unless I do.

If doubt and fear arise...
I won't let them in. My vision's too strong to let negativity win.

THIS WILL ALL BE WORTH IT...

I will manifest my goals. My dreams are getting closer. I feel it in my soul.

EVALUATE & ADAPT: TRACK YOUR PROGRESS

You made a commitment – to your goals, to your vision, to yourself. Monitoring your progress is the only way to know if you're keeping that commitment. It's the only way to know where you are in relation to where you want to be. Each day, you'll need to look yourself in the mirror and objectively answer one question: *did I make progress toward my goals today?*

If the answer is *yes*, that's great. Pat yourself on the back, but don't get complacent. It will take a series of these small wins to secure the big win, which is achieving your vision. If the answer is *no*, that's okay – the world won't end. Instead of engaging in negative self-talk or beating yourself up about it, direct your energy toward reflecting on why you didn't make progress. Figure out what you need to do differently so that a singular *no* doesn't turn into a string of them. Adapt your approach.

Each of your goals is measurable and time-bound, which means you can set benchmarks to measure your progress against your timeline. Note that benchmarks might overlap and, as you track your progress, some may need to be adjusted or moved.

Use the example on the next page to help you create benchmarks for your goals.

Sample Benchmarks

- **Goal:** By the end of the year, secure a new job that improves my current salary.
- **Timeline:** Six months
- **Benchmarks**
  - Month 1: Devote two hours per week to job-searching.
  - Month 2: Attend local networking events + job fairs.
  - Months 3-4: Submit at least five applications/month.
  - Month 5: Secure at least three interviews.
  - Month 6: Receive a job offer.

While benchmarks are key to staying consistent, so are other accountability mechanisms – including people. There's so much value in a human support system. Have a person who will tell it to you straight when you're not following through. Identify someone who's willing to be a supportive listener when you need to vent. If possible, find that mover-and-shaker who can connect you to a broader network of people who can help you. Whatever you do, ensure you have someone who can be there for you on the journey.

As you evaluate how things are going, remember two things:

1. **Success is a series of small wins.**
   This journey is yours, so you've got to be your biggest supporter. Recognize and celebrate the triumphs you experience along the way and use them as motivation to keep progressing.

2. **Don't give up before the miracle happens.**
   There'll be times when the journey feels tough and lonely. You will absolutely stumble. If you don't, are you even growing? To fail, you have to have tried in the first place. Keep that in mind and know that you can get back up and regain control.

Celebrating the good and remaining focused in the midst of the bad motivates you to stay in action, which is the most critical part of this whole journey. Even when you take two steps backward, three to the side, or aren't making any movement at all, know that you have a plan (your goals!) and the power to put one foot in front of the other to progress.

The Bottom Line: Evaluating your progress is the only way you'll know if you're on the right track. To do this, you'll need to learn how to balance being your own biggest supporter while simultaneously being your own toughest critic. When you fall short, remember that you have a plan – reference it, pick up where you left off, and keep pushing forward!

You can do it.

Benchmarks – Quarter 1

Reference your goals on pages 42-46. Since they were written using the SMART approach, each one should be time-bound and measurable. With your timeline and measures in mind, write down the benchmarks you think you need to accomplish this quarter to get closer to your goals.

Goal 1
-
-
-

Goal 2
-
-
-

Goal 3
-
-
-

Goal 4
-
-
-

Goal 5
-
-
-

Progress Tracker – Month 1

what are some of the feelings you experienced this month?

what benchmarks did you reach? Which ones fell short?

what obstacles or missteps did you encounter?

How do you need to tweak your approach moving forward?

what would you like to achieve by the end of next month?

Progress Tracker – Month 2

What are some of the feelings you experienced this month?

Look back at your Month 1 Tracker – did you achieve what you hoped you would this month?

What benchmarks did you reach? Which ones fell short?

What obstacles or missteps did you encounter?

How do you need to tweak your approach moving forward?

What would you like to achieve by the end of next month?

Progress Tracker – Month 3

What are some of the feelings you experienced this month?

Look back at your Month 2 Tracker – did you achieve what you hoped you would this month?

What benchmarks did you reach? Which ones fell short?

What obstacles or missteps did you encounter?

How do you need to tweak your approach moving forward?

What would you like to achieve by the end of next month?

Benchmarks – Quarter 2

Reference the benchmarks you set in Quarter 1 (page 67). Based on your progress, update or add new benchmarks here. Don't forget to keep your goal timing and measures in mind.

Goal 1

-
-
-

Goal 2

-
-
-

Goal 3

-
-
-

Goal 4

-
-
-

Goal 5

-
-
-

Progress Tracker – Month 4

What are some of the feelings you experienced this month?

Look back at your Month 3 Tracker – did you achieve what you hoped you would this month?

What benchmarks did you reach? Which ones fell short?

What obstacles or missteps did you encounter?

How do you need to tweak your approach moving forward?

What would you like to achieve by the end of next month?

Progress Tracker – Month 5

What are some of the feelings you experienced this month?

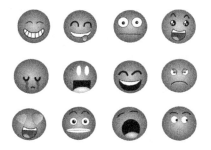

Look back at your Month 4 Tracker – did you achieve what you hoped you would this month?

What benchmarks did you reach? Which ones fell short?

What obstacles or missteps did you encounter?

How do you need to tweak your approach moving forward?

What would you like to achieve by the end of next month?

Progress Tracker – Month 6

What are some of the feelings you experienced this month?

Look back at your Month 5 Tracker – did you achieve what you hoped you would this month?

What benchmarks did you reach? Which ones fell short?

What obstacles or missteps did you encounter?

How do you need to tweak your approach moving forward?

What would you like to achieve by the end of next month?

Benchmarks – Quarter 3

Reference the benchmarks you set in Quarter 2 (page 71). Based on your progress, update or add new benchmarks here. Don't forget to keep your goal timing and measures in mind.

Goal 1
-
-
-

Goal 2
-
-
-

Goal 3
-
-
-

Goal 4
-
-
-

Goal 5
-
-
-

Progress Tracker – Month 7

What are some of the feelings you experienced this month?

Look back at your Month 6 Tracker – did you achieve what you hoped you would this month?

What benchmarks did you reach? Which ones fell short?

What obstacles or missteps did you encounter?

How do you need to tweak your approach moving forward?

What would you like to achieve by the end of next month?

Progress Tracker – Month 8

What are some of the feelings you experienced this month?

Look back at your Month 7 Tracker – did you achieve what you hoped you would this month?

What benchmarks did you reach? Which ones fell short?

What obstacles or missteps did you encounter?

How do you need to tweak your approach moving forward?

What would you like to achieve by the end of next month?

Progress Tracker – Month 9

What are some of the feelings you experienced this month?

Look back at your Month 8 Tracker – did you achieve what you hoped you would this month?

What benchmarks did you reach? Which ones fell short?

What obstacles or missteps did you encounter?

How do you need to tweak your approach moving forward?

What would you like to achieve by the end of next month?

Benchmarks – Quarter 4

Reference the benchmarks you set in Quarter 3 (page 75). Based on your progress, update or add new benchmarks here. Don't forget to keep your goal timing and measures in mind.

Goal 1

-
-
-

Goal 2

-
-
-

Goal 3

-
-
-

Goal 4

-
-
-

Goal 5

-
-
-

Progress Tracker – Month 10

What are some of the feelings you experienced this month?

Look back at your Month 9 Tracker – did you achieve what you hoped you would this month?

What benchmarks did you reach? Which ones fell short?

What obstacles or missteps did you encounter?

How do you need to tweak your approach moving forward?

What would you like to achieve by the end of next month?

Progress Tracker – Month 11

What are some of the feelings you experienced this month?

Look back at your Month 10 Tracker – did you achieve what you hoped you would this month?

What benchmarks did you reach? Which ones fell short?

What obstacles or missteps did you encounter?

How do you need to tweak your approach moving forward?

What would you like to achieve by the end of next month?

Progress Tracker – Month 12

What are some of the feelings you experienced this month?

Look back at your Month 11 Tracker – did you achieve what you hoped you would this month?

What benchmarks did you reach? Which ones fell short?

What obstacles or missteps did you encounter?

If you've achieved your goals, how does it feel? What did you learn about yourself?

If you have more work to do toward your goals, how will you tweak your approach moving forward?

A Final Word

Regardless of what happens on your journey to manifest your goals and reach your dreams, you should be proud of yourself. I'm proud of you.

You were bold enough to say you had a dream. You were wise enough to put a plan together to pursue that dream. Most importantly, you love yourself enough to believe you can make it a reality.

I hope *Dream with Intention* serves as a guiding light for you to follow on your journey to manifestation. I hope my words made you feel prepared. To believe in yourself. To be strategic. To do what you can with what you have. To recognize struggle and discomfort as a sign of transformation. To embrace failure as an opportunity for growth.

You are breaking the current mold of your life to reshape it into a vision that brings you closer to your dreams. Surrender to the unknown, get comfortable with the uncomfortable, find your greatness in the struggle, and don't quit. You didn't spend time developing a plan only to abandon it. Always remember that you are in control.

Thank you for trusting me to help you manifest your goals.

May you grow, may you evolve, and may you live out your dreams.

Coach Coco B.

Dream with Intention

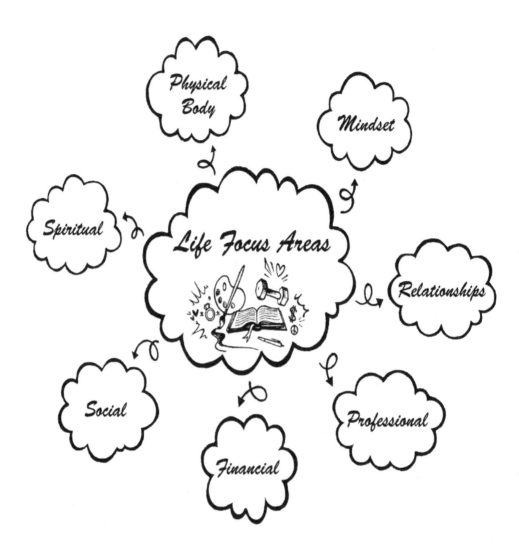

ABOUT THE AUTHOR

Mariko Bennett is the Founder and President of COCO B. Productions, a premier consulting firm for corporate, government, and nonprofit sectors. Providing tailored advisory in the areas of business strategy, fundraising, event and production management, and advertising solutions, she is deeply passionate about positioning companies and individuals for long-term, sustainable success. She epitomizes catching lightning in a bottle, and to know her is to be acquainted with the raw power of possibility, courage, and perseverance.

Once a leading external and political affairs executive with almost two decades of verifiable success, Mariko has represented Fortune 500 companies on Capitol Hill and in the corporate sector, managed political action committees, led communications initiatives, and developed effective long-term inclusion and diversity engagement strategies with minority advocacy groups. Through her extensive track record, she has consistently shattered glass ceilings and broken through societal and self-imposed barriers.

In 2017, after spending a few months weighing the risks and rewards of entrepreneurship, Mariko took the leap of faith and founded her own consulting firm. Trading the comforts of the corporate world for the uncertainties of entrepreneurship came with hard-hitting challenges, but like the true fighter she is, Mariko conquered every obstacle with passion and fortitude. She coupled her education and experience with business acumen and unwavering resilience to build COCO B. Productions from the ground up into a buzzing global enterprise. Today, Mariko trail blazes as a creative thought leader in leadership coaching, and personal growth and development, guiding hundreds of clients through her riveting "C-Power" vision-boarding method that Crystalizes, Customizes, Cultivates, and Curates your dreams into reality. Her mega-client portfolio includes

Fortune 500 companies and international influencers she has worked with to identify their motivations, and empower them to succeed through changes in psychology, attitudes, and habits.

Driven by her, "Do More. Do Better. No Excuses." motto, Mariko is also recognized for her leadership and impact in the community. She currently serves on the Corporate Advisory Council for the Congressional Black Caucus Foundation, Inc. where she supports programs that further the CBCF's mission to advance the global black community by developing leaders, informing policy, and educating the public. She is also a chartering member of the Metropolitan Washington, D.C. Chapter of the National Coalition of 100 Black Women, Inc. where she serves as the 1st Vice President of programs. She is a dedicated member of The Links, Inc. where she serves as the Co-Chair of International Trends and Services and Chair of the Social Committee.

In addition to being an entrepreneur and thought-leader, Mariko is a wife, mother of three, author, and podcast host. As a dreamer and serial goal-setter, she aims to continuously push the boundary of the possible and is energized by the prospect of helping people self-actualize their potential.

Mariko holds a Bachelor of Arts (Communications) degree from the University of Maryland Global Campus.

Mariko enjoys spending time with her husband, Randy, and her three children, Christian, Ethan, and McKenzie.

CONNECT WITH MARIKO!

www.instagram.com/cocobproduction

www.facebook.com/cocobproductions

www.linkedin.com/in/mariko-bennett

www.marikobennett.com

Made in the USA
Columbia, SC
27 October 2022

70091937R00050